WoW
(Words of Wisdom)

Addo Anyani-Boadum

ISBN: 098643261X
ISBN 13: 9780986432613

CONTENTS

CONTENTS

I dedicate this book to three categories of people whose diverse roles, through the help of the Almighty God, have brought me to a pedestal while I am still rising.

To Mama and Dada, who nurtured me and taught me since my childhood, and are, at the same time, my spiritual father and mother in the Lord. Thank you for your continued prayers.

To my loving wife, Lesley, and our beautiful girls, Mikaela, Isabel, and Daniela, who have been great treasures and true helpers to me in full-time ministry.

To my siblings, Dr. Oheneba and family; Kristodea and family; Chief and family; and Nicky and family. Thank you very much for always being there for me.

ACKNOWLEDGMENTS

My primary acknowledgment goes to the Almighty God and the Holy Spirit for accepting me and giving me an opportunity to be a blessing to the world.

I wish to thank the following people who have contributed to this rewarding project. With selfless nights and communications, you brought out the best in me as I wrote this book.

My heartfelt and deepest appreciation goes to:

The Rt. Rev. Dr. Nana Anyani-Boadum and your team for the proofreading, editing, guidance, and continued support.

My wife, Lesley, who worked through the initial scripts and did some transcribing. For your grammatical checks, thank you.

Michael Boadi for a great design, website, and cover layout.

The Rev. Titi Lartey for the publishing referrals.

Nana Kwabena Anyani-Boadum (Chief) for documenting information for the website and social media.

The Rev. Dr. Oheneba Anyani-Boadum for reviews on publishing options and guidance.

Thank you all.

FOREWORD

When the American poet Emily Dickinson wrote, "I know nothing in the world that has as much power as a word," she was only confirming what the wise man said in Proverbs 18:21: *Death and life are in the power of the tongue: and they that love it shall eat the fruit thereof.* Genesis 1:1–3 spells out how the universe was created by a word from the mouth of God:

In the beginning God created the heaven and the earth. And the earth was without form, and void; and darkness was upon the face of the deep. And the Spirit of God moved upon the face of the waters. And God said, "Let there be light: and there was light."

Words, whether spoken or written, carry immeasurable significance because words have a direct impact on the human soul. Words have the power to captivate and control our emotions. We laugh because of what others tell us. We cry because of what we hear. We change moods in an instant because of messages we receive from relatives, friends, or neighbors. That is why words must be used properly and in the right contexts; otherwise, they can cause havoc or disharmony to those who read or hear them. However, an edifying word brings joy and hope to those who need it most.

The apostle Paul gave profound advice in Ephesians 4:29: *Do not let any unwholesome talk come out of your mouths, but only what is helpful for building others up according to their needs, that it may benefit those who listen.* In this instructive book, *Words Of Wisdom,* the Rev. Otumfuo Addo Anyani-Boadum has laid out principles on how to harness our tongues appropriately as we strive to define ourselves within the context of human personality, by having the positive fruits of the tongue.

My wish for you is that the words in this book will not lose their ethos or credibility, but they will make a positive impact in your life.

To the Rev. Otumfuo Addo Anyani-Boadum, congratulations.

The Rt. Rev. Dr. Nana Anyani-Boadum (ThB, ThM, ThD), superintendent bishop of Jesus Generation Ministries

* Council Member of Regent University College of Science and Technology

* Executive Member of Ghana Pentecostal and Charismatics Council

* Chairman of the National Coalition for Proper Human Sexual and Family Behaviour

* Eminent West African

INTRODUCTION

Life is built on words. In the beginning, God created the whole world with words from His mouth. By the spoken words of God, the world, which was without form, became a beautiful and orderly place.

With words, He called into being all creatures, plants, and animals. By the spoken word from the very mouth of God, the whole universe came into being. He formed Adam and Eve and breathed life into their nostrils, and they became living souls. Today we are all the result of God's creation. We owe our lives to this great God.

Words can make or break you, especially if you are a public figure with the media spotlight on you. The Bible declares that you shall have and experience whatever you say. The Bible also declares that life and death are in the power of the tongue. Use your tongue and your mouth to profess and establish what you want to see in your life, work, family, career, and aspirations.

As you read this book, you will gain more understanding and insight into how you need to chart your life's journey by using words of power, knowledge, and understanding.

As you declare and confess these words, you will see tremendous changes in your life, business, organisation, church, or any field you find yourself in. God bless you.

Chapter One

The Power of Words

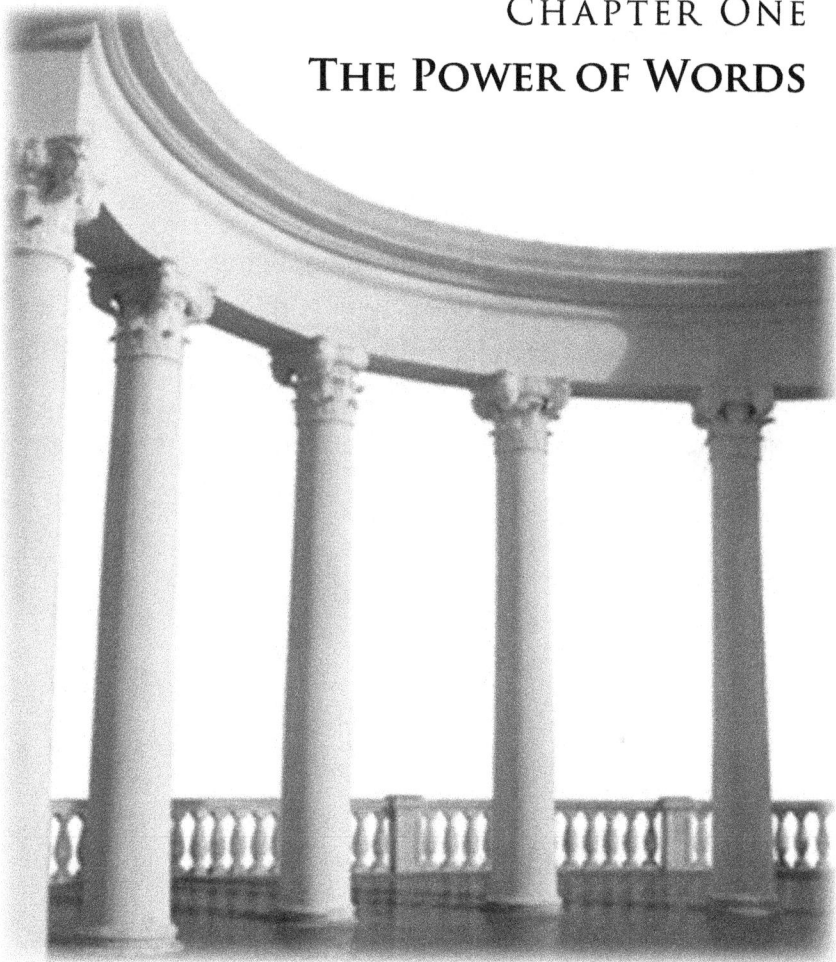

You can chart your life—your visions, dreams, goals, and aspirations—and those of your family and loved ones with the very words you speak. You can be what you want to be, and you can also undo anything you desire not to see or have. All of this is possible if you learn how to use your mouth to speak what you want.

You can agree with your children, your partner, your family, and your friends on what you want by all speaking the same thing in unison, and it shall come to pass in your lives.

Words are a spirit and carry an power within them. If you choose the right words, the power within those words is activated to your benefit.

Seek the truth and sell it not. Welcome to a new phase of your life.

CHAPTER TWO

LIFE, FAITH, AND GOD

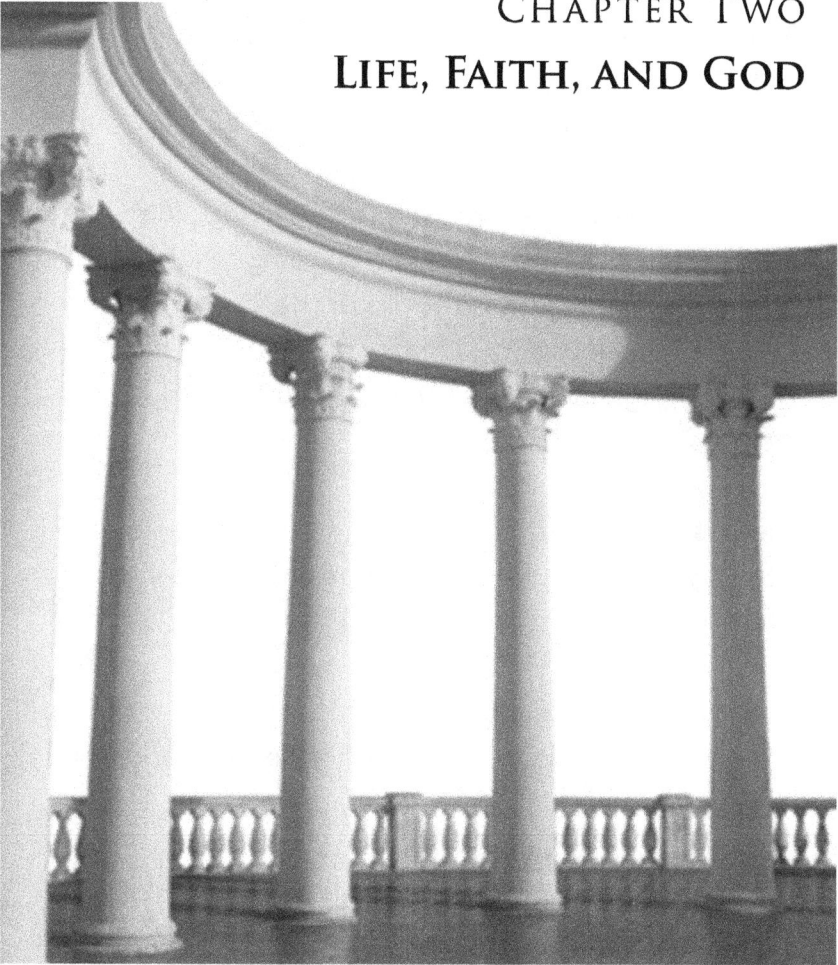

A life of gladness is all that your Creator expects of you, and for that reason, you receive upon your life the oil of gladness.

We live to fulfill that life of gladness. You have to do certain things in order to realize your life of gladness.

A life of gladness is an established life. It is the life that knows what it requires. The life of gladness has a preset agenda, needs, and planning beforehand.

The life of gladness is the life of the Christian missionary. The life of gladness means fulfilling what is on the Master's agenda. This is the life of the soul-winner.

This life of gladness depends on your attitude toward the mission of Christ on earth.

The basis of faith is fundamentally centered on one key rule: in whom you put your personal reliance and absolute trust, confidence, and belief.

Faith is personal. Faith has everything to do with *you*. Depend on faith for your uncapped income and abundance. Depend on faith for your answers.

Faith, when held onto, will break all manner of traditions. Faith does not respect norms or natural laws.

You have a personal responsibility to build your faith and have it work for you. If you are not getting the desired results, it means your faith is not being fully utilised. If it is, faith it will surely work.

Remember, though, that faith is denying all other options and staying unmovable with God.

Believing is seeing beyond the physical. Believing is placing all of your confidence in God.

You require faith to stay in this world of fragility. The world is so fragile that you cannot live in it without faith. Faith is what gives you balance and stability in this world.

If you want your faith to bring the unseen and the supernatural into your life and that of your family, you cannot afford to stay stagnant. Seek for more insight.

Learn to declare your greatness; learn to declare your victories. Use your mouth to declare favor, increase, grace, power, and success. Use your mouth to declare your faith in God.

Declare yourself out of the problem; declare yourself out of that pain and sickness. Declare victory.

Worship brings the atmosphere of faith and miracles. Worship activates the God mode.

The moment you activate the God mode through praise and worship, negative things begin to give way instantly. God and His presence dwell in an atmosphere of worship and praise.

Knowing that God has confidence in you, you need to have faith in God first and then in yourself.

Just because the first business did not work does not mean a new one is going to fail. No, it will not. Have faith and exercise it greatly in the Lord.

For every question, doubt, or challenge that you have, knowing where to get the answer will determine whether it can be resolved.

Wisdom is the ability to apply knowledge correctly and be dominant in a particular field or area. The ability to identify exactly what you are seeking is pivotal. Not knowing what you are seeking puts you in a position of not being able to find it.

A treasure, when discovered, is priceless.

Jumping from person to person and asking ignorant people in your state of confusion and uncertainty can result in disaster.

The manner in which you seek can result in either trouble or a desired answer.

Seeking requires having an agenda.

What is your reaction the moment you find what you have been looking for?

Seeing and *beholding* are two different things. To *see* is natural. To *behold* is seeing beyond the natural.

Seeking goes beyond assumptions.

Your life must be consumed with the preoccupation of looking for God.

The presence of the word *but* immediately informs us that certain things have previously been mentioned.

But also serves as a caution about those previously mentioned things.

But informs us to be aware of what is to come or has yet to be stated.

But also tells us that the coming words or impending statement is in contrast with the former.

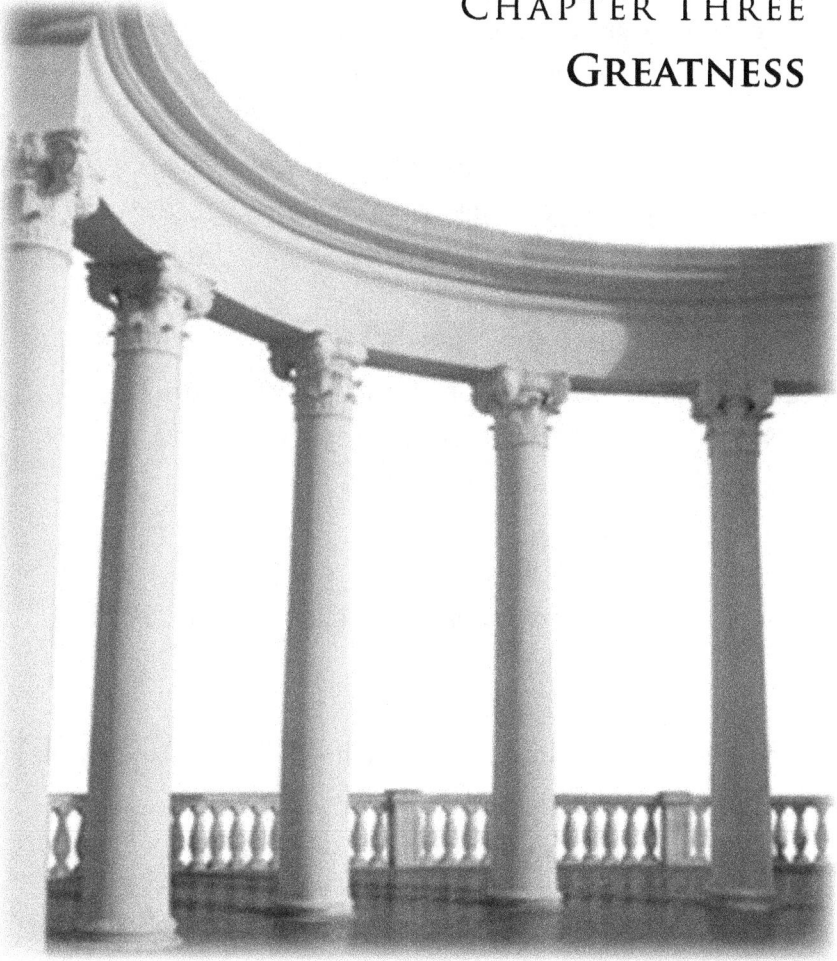

The path of greatness is a path of discipline and studying.

Greatness is a journey.

Greatness is a road that starts from one point and leads to a place of fulfillment.

A person that attains true greatness is a successful person.

Greatness is when your impact and influence now stretch beyond your personal feelings, your actions, your thoughts, your personality, your titles, and your certificates.

Greatness is when your impact and influence help change people's mind-set and their way of living, talk, lifestyle, environment, and decisions; it gives people a true meaning to life.

Becoming great or becoming a success does not happen by mere words.

Becoming great is more than having a doctorate degree or being called the most decorated statesman.

The best unbiased recipe for greatness is the Word of God.

If your chosen recipe for greatness is outside the Word of God, then your greatness may not stand the test of time.

The ground on which you build is very important, and this foundation will determine the extent of your greatness. Make the Word of God your foundation for greatness. Your greatness must be linked to a source, and you must always respect your source.

Your greatness needs to be linked to someone greater.

Your greatness must have a reference point.

If you want to be great but don't know God, then the impact of your greatness will be limited or, in some cases, will be of no effect.

You cannot be the greatest musician, writer, teacher, manufacturer, engineer, developer, business entrepreneur, or prophet of God if you don't know God.

The moment you have more than one source, you dilute the process of your greatness.

On the journey to greatness, you will face obstacles.

The making of greatness come with some challenges along the journey, and you must learn to be strong and of good courage.

Don't walk away from Christianity because you have not yet received the answer to that issue you have been praying about.

If you want to be great, you need to know who you are.

The recipe to greatness is the consistent, daily routine of studying the Word of God and meditating on it.

You keep talking about greatness, you keep talking about changing your current job, moving to a new house, buying a new car, or moving to the top, but you are still doing things in the same old ways. Greatness comes with a desire to change.

Your worth is in your obedience.

Greatness comes with patience.

The road to greatness also requires restraint. Your ability to restrain yourself can aid you on your road to greatness.

Be very careful because your friends and the people you call companions can help make or break your journey to greatness.

In order to be great and have greatness, you must seek guidance from God.

In finding greatness, you must wait for God to talk to you.

Greatness does not come by lying in bed every day.

Change your attitude.

Stop being lazy if you want to be great.

Greatness requires education.

Greatness requires planning.

To be great, you must be happy with what you have; seek change if it's not sufficient or what you expect.

Greatness requires love.

You cannot be great if you tend to dislike people without cause.

Greatness is not complete until it's acknowledged by the multitudes.

Greatness strives to be the best.

Greatness has a mind-set.

People may react to you the way they do because they see you as a threat.

Your divine destiny and results lay in your realisation that God has far better plans for you than your parents ever dreamed for you.

You are not just any ordinary creation. You are not a biological error.

Your awareness of truth can immediately change your position.

God will not stand by, unconcerned about your situation, until you have your desired results and outcome.

You are not what people think you are.

People do not yet know the magnitude and glorious honor that you have.

People have used your present disposition to stigmatize you, but God is using it to transform you to the next level.

CHAPTER FOUR
LOVE, OBEDIENCE, AND SUDDEN MOMENTS

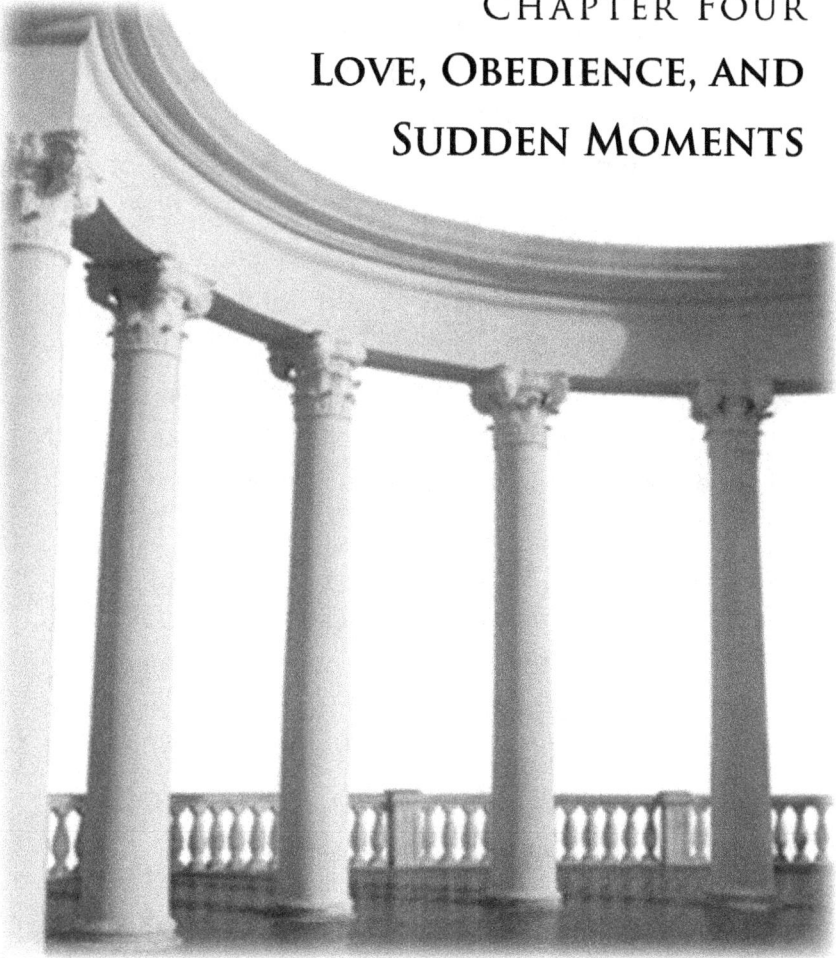

L ove has no beginning, and love has no end.

People will react to love and anything that can impact or cause them to lose love.

Until your sacrifice costs you, then you have not attained the full expression of love.

Jesus' position on the cross was your place to be, the pain was meant to be your pain, but He took it for your sake, that you might have life and have it to the fullest. Yet with all of this, you are not giving Him back the love required of you.

Don't prostitute the love of God. If you can take pride in work over church, then your love is not complete.

Obedience is not tagged only to people who are superior to you. Obedience is obedience only when you explicitly follow a checklist for whatever instruction you were told without deviating.

The difference between the successful, the poor, the rich, and the person getting 100 percent and the one getting 5 percent could be a result of their reaction to instruction.

Society has a lot to offer, but you need to know what you want and how you go about getting it.

Your obedience is going to be the unique key to your fulfillment. What you need to unlock your life to the next phase is obedience.

Partial obedience is disobedience.

The key to activating your blessings and the supernatural is **obedience**.

- In obeying, you trust the instructor.

- In obeying, you follow the instructions.

- Obedience is when you don't question but just act spontaneously.

- In obeying, you act promptly.

- In obeying, you often have to let go of your best. Letting go does not mean losing. Whenever you let go, you automatically let God in, and God will fill up any vacuum that must have been created. When you let go, Heaven releases what's there for you.

- In obeying, you have to release what you have in your hand in order to activate your blessings and the supernatural.

- You must give away your valuables.

Obedience is worship.

- In obeying, you don't change course.

  - Follow the path.

  - Your obedience to the path will lead you to your greatness and blessings.

If life becomes an experiment, you will take chances with real opportunities and, by doing so, miss your miracle.

Your life is valuable and priceless. Nothing in this world can replace your life once lost or damaged.

You may come across opportunities, and your reaction and attitude to those opportunities will determine if such will land again on your doorstep or timeline.

The fact that people have mocked you, even when you try different options and consistently pray but have not yet received your desired answer, does not mean God has forsaken you.

The fact that things don't seem to be going very well for you or your family is not an indication that your situation will not change for the better.

A sometimes missed opportunity is not a sign that it was never meant to be yours.

When the going gets tough and the road seems blurred, take some time to pause, reflect, regroup, and seek more of God to give you light for the rest of the journey.

No matter what you may be facing in life, there is a time when suddenly something happens, and it breaks the cycle of events. Suddenly something extraordinary happens, and your tears immediately turn into joy.

The sudden moments are controlled by God the Almighty.

There are no formulas with which the sudden moments occur.

The sudden moments are timings and moments of God the Almighty.

The sudden moments have nothing to do with you; they are initiated by the Spirit of God for your personal change in the circumstance and to His glory.

The moment of your discovery and realisation of the truth is the moment of your miracle and the turn-around of your life.

You are a global publication in a special way.

You are too expensive to allow the devil to mess around with your mind, your thoughts, your ideas, your children, your job, your health, your business, your home, your ministry, your occupation, and anything that concerns you.

Who you are and everything concerning your life was spoken by God's own mouth and written in the Bible. The Good Book says, I preplanned your Path and re-created you. Be the best wherever you are.

Greatness in God's Glory

The mind of man can never conceive the totality of the unfathomable Jehovah.

When you encounter the glory of God, it will blow your mind, your thoughts, and your perceptions about the magnitude of the glory of God.

After an encounter with the glory of God, if you had the rest of your life, you would never finish talking about the glory of God that you have seen.

The glory makes up for your shortfall.

Embedded in the glory of God is the grace of God.

Embedded in the glory of God is the power of God.

Embedded in the glory of God is healing. Embedded in the glory of God is all you need.

The glory of God may be the missing factor in your life.

In the glory of God is the presence of God.

The glory of God is your lifeline and life-support machine.

In the glory of God is also the voice of God. When the glory of God comes, it brings you direction.

The place of prayer is where divinity meets with humanity.

In the place of prayer, our language is consistent and uniform.

Learn the the vital modalities around prayer. Just as not knowing the full instructions of a manual or an item can damage that item or cause harm to you.

Use your prayer to your advantage.

Don't gamble your options at the place of prayer.

In the place of prayer, God demands that we listen.

The Power of "Today" and Belief

Your **today** is the full realisation of a spiritual word declared by God's Spirit early on.

Spoken words are the creation of structures in the realm of the Spirit.

Every word is spirit, and the spirit of the word backs the word to actualise its existence.

Your actions between the space of actualisation, the gestation period, and waiting determine much of your life today.

Today is your opportunity to use the power of the spoken word and cause change to take place.

Today is your time to change the things that are wrong in your world.

In believing, you do not doubt.

In believing, you do not question why and how.

In believing, you do not set a timeline.

In believing, you don't listen to any opinions.

In believing, you don't look to your natural senses and self.

In believing, you do not shift your gaze.

In believing, you keep your focus.

In believing, you are resilient in your faith!

In believing, you not only keep hope alive, but you go further. Hope is the expectation for something to become a reality. Believing becomes, "I have it! And I knew I had it."

Acceptance and ownership are totally different.

Maybe you believed something and accepted that, *but you didn't own it*. That is the biggest problem. Don't just accept but accept ownership.

Confession is not just saying it, but it also requires that you believe it, say it consistently with your mouth, and do it; live in that world until it becomes a reality.

CHAPTER FIVE

THE POWER OF GIFTS

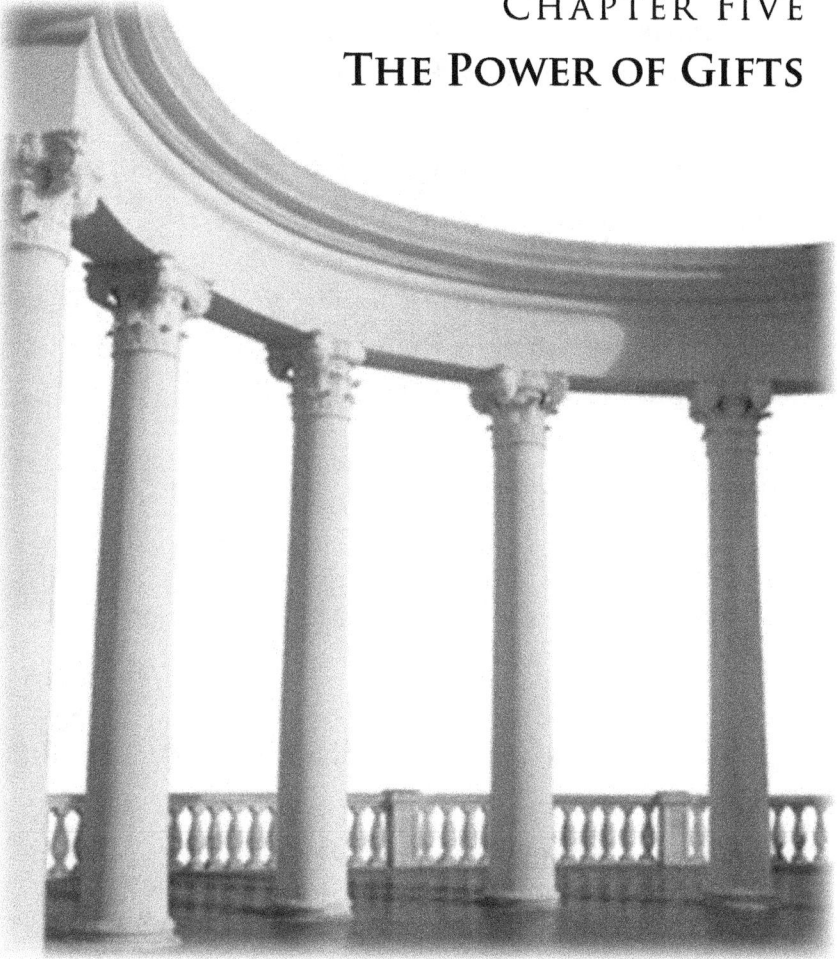

The presence of a gift must be valued.

Certain openings or opportunities will be open to you (conditionally) only if you have a gift to offer.

The arms of the world love to embrace only the people with a gift.

The discovery of the world's hidden potentials and treasures can only be birthed by the gifted.

The life we live will become colorless and stagnant without possessing a gift.

If you do not have a gift in your life, your life becomes stagnant in the sense that you are not maximising the full potential of your given life.

Any life that is underutilised can be traced to a gift not discovered.

Underutilised lives are the result of untapped and unrealised gifts.

Success, therefore, is the result of a discovered and utilised gift.

As a world, we cannot be where we are now if gifts were not given and discovered.

The true extent of your potential can be reached only through the discovery of your gift.

A gift is a precious item in the eyes of its giver.

You are not the creator of your gift. Gifts have a source. Every gift can be traced to its source.

Any gift that is not traceable is spurious. If your gift is not traceable, then it's stolen.

The giver of the gift values that gift, even if you have no regard for it.

The number-one step in identifying your gift is identifying its source.

When you realise that God is your source and the reason for your very existence, you can then go to Him and enquire about your gift and the assignment for which you are living.

Every human in this world was born with a gift to accomplish his or her assignment and benefit the church and the world.

Your gift needs to bless others and bring change to situations.

Your gift needs to create new things for you and others.

It's not a gift if it's not been put to use.

A gift is only useful when utilised in the hand of the possessor.

A gift satisfies a need. A gift always bridges a chasm.

You need to know your gift.

You need to locate your gift.

Your gift is not only beneficial to you, but also to people around the world. Your laziness in not discovering your gift deprives millions of people of treasures. If you don't care, think about what you may be doing to others.

Knowing your gift is the beginning of your success. Do all you can to identify and locate your gift because an identified gift brings blessings and dispels scarcity. A gift defined gives light.

The saying, "There is a light at the end of the tunnel," is not necessarily true. Rather, your gift will bring light at the end of the tunnel.

Going through the tunnel of life without a gift is darkness.

If the gift you have leads people to make errors, brings deception, and destroys families and lives, instead of bringing satisfaction, then that gift is not from God.

When your gift becomes visible, the world will want to know you. When your gift becomes visible and transferable, your greatness comes. Whenever your gift is made apparent, people immediately begin to see you differently. When your gift is visible and impacts lives, people's perception of you and all that concerns you automatically changes.

The expressions and communication of your gift will automatically open doors to you.

You need to know how to present yourself in order for your gift to open doors for you.

Presenting yourself correctly and appropriately is the key.

With your current composure and mannerisms, certain doors cannot open to you. And if per chance you are permitted in, your mannerisms and presentation will bring you back out. This is a word of wisdom.

Don't stay in your arrogance and think that because you have a gift you can remain at the top. Very soon you will be forced out or replaced.

You also need to know the conditions under which your gift can be accepted.

Your gift when discovered, utilized, and developed will bring you fruitfulness.

You can only actualize your gift if you know your source. Don't disrespect your source.

Your gift is connected to your source. Your gift will bring you before leaders and nations.

Your gift will place you in authority.

Your gift is connected to the doors of your life.

Stepping into a door of your life at the wrong time can lead to delays and difficulties.

When you enter into the room that your gift caused to open, know when to exit. Don't overstay because that could be detrimental to the next higher level of your life.

Every door of your life brings a new opportunity and potential challenges; therefore, be mindful of the seasons in your life.

Your gift makes room for you, and each room comes with a season.

When your gift makes room for you, even when no opportunity remains or every area is saturated, the fact that you have discovered your gift and know how to use it means that there will be room for you in that given situation or place.

There is power in the gift that you have. The gift carries within it its power. Your awareness of this breaks all limitations that will be presented to the gift.

Your gift shall preserve you and your posterity.

Your gift is connected to your glory.

Don't leave this earth without discovering your gift, developing your gift, and utilising your gift to become a blessing to others and yourself.

CHAPTER SIX

WAITING AND WORSHIP

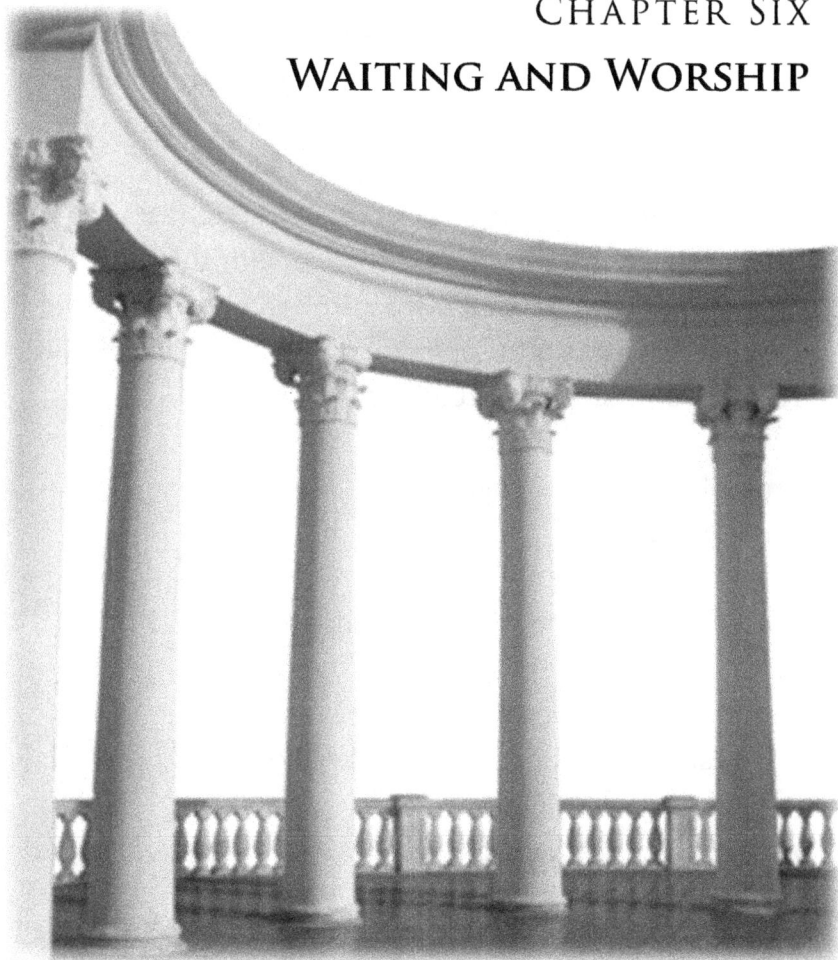

Time is the most important currency and attribute in the world.

My consistency with God is not determined or measured by my walking into the church day in and day out. It's about my fellowship with the Father.

Fellowship is a deeper bond than just having a relationship. We need to move from just having a relationship to engaging in fellowship.

Consistency is not about ticking boxes; consistency is doing the right thing in consonance with the Word of God. It is saying the same thing repeatedly in spite of the circumstances and confessing what God Himself will confess for that given situation.

Time plays a crucial role in your life. If you want something, you need to make time for it.

The essence of time cannot be underestimated.

In the processing of time, there is an element of waiting. Waiting is as important as timing. Knowing when to wait, and when not to wait, is crucial throughout the years of your life as well as in your daily activities.

You can wait in the queue to be served at the post office, but when it comes to waiting on God or His Word, people don't have time.

Your moment of victory can always be described as the coming to an end of a season.

You can only say, "I'm waiting" when you have already completed something.

Expectancy carries a desire to receive something or somebody special. You cannot be expectant of something and not have a desire for it.

Waiting brings about the next stage, called expectancy. At the expectancy stage, you are in a ready mood.

Waiting does not mean to sit still.

You can't say you are waiting if you have not planted, invested, or done anything.

If you are waiting and don't do anything about your waiting, you will not get any results.

If you don't water and till the ground in the waiting season, you won't get any harvest.

Waiting can be lonely, but be careful not to start murmuring and blaming people.

You must be willing to trust God through your season of waiting.

In your season of waiting, continuously pray in the Spirit.

Waiting requires you to be alert and vigilant.

Waiting on God means to stay in an expectant mood.

During your waiting period, don't miss your set time, which is determined by God. That is your due season.

Waiting without anticipation gives you no results.

To your waiting add prayer and expectancy; continued sowing and patience; and studying the Word of God.

If you wait correctly on God, He will teach you how to rest and be fulfilled.

Worship is part of fulfilling your service.

In accomplishing any duty of service, regardless of who you give the service to, demonstrating the act of reverence or worship is an integral part.

Worship births loyalty. A true worshipper is a loyal member. Worship comes with a cost.

A true worshipper is a discerner.

In giving your worship, make sure it goes to God your Creator and the Giver of your life.

What situation is blocking your worship? You cannot give your worship to any man, woman, or object except God the Almighty.

People love objects and articles of Christianity but not God Himself. Why should someone be interested in worshipping the created rather than the Creator?

If you worship truly, you can easily build a relationship with the Holy Spirit.

Worshipping in spirit and in truth is the giving of worship regardless of the situation and the people around you.

It is in worship that the Spirit of God moves mostly. In worship his presence is felt and known. When you worship, you see the totality of God's magnitude. Your perception of His magnitude is enlarged as you worship Him.

Worship opens doors. If you can worship Him, doors in your life shall open. Worship is communication. A true worshipper is a good communicator.

Worship began and is still continuing in Heaven.

Even the beasts mentioned in the book of Revelation understood why they needed to worship. They fell down on seeing God lift up the book.

Why is it challenging for you to accept him and worhip.

Worship requires speaking forth appellations to the Creator to show who He is, what He does, and to honor Him.

Have you become too pious in your gowns, your other dresses, your position, your wealth, and your assets, even when it comes to worshipping the One who created you? Do you find it too challenging to lie down or prostrate yourself in your designer suit or dress? Be careful.

Worship goes beyond your traditional senses and feelings.

The most important thing to remember is that the picture and description of Heaven that you have read in the Bible is accurate, true, present, and very real.

Take moments of your time and join in worship with Heaven and its hosts. It is an unspeakable experience.

When you open your heart to worship, you can experience the power of God through it.

When you worship, you receive restoration. When you worship, you receive direction from God. Worship brings you answers to your requests. Whenever you worship God, you get a response.

In worship, you receive healing.

If you will seek Him through worship, you will find Him because He is also seeking those who are seeking Him.

You must present a substance in worship. It can be time, skill, prayer, love, seed, money, or singing, all to God.

You do not go to a king empty handed. You must have a gift in your hand, and it must be valuable and precious to you.

You must know the worth of God when you go to Him in worship. This is what the twenty-four elders and the four creatures in Heaven know. This is what this Syrophoenician woman knew.

This is what David knew when he danced before God; it never mattered to David who he was. David didn't care what throne he was sitting on, what apparel he was wearing, what he was worth, or what perception his kingdom had of him. He was more concerned about how he would be able to please his Father, the Creator and great God. He wanted to give Him the best of worship.

Your moments of worship must be just as dear to you and must not be exchanged for anything else.

You cannot buy back the time lost in worship.

The key to all that you want and need is worship.

Our worship is always directed to a source. The source receiving your worship is very important. There is one source and several outlets. It is your duty to personally locate that singular source and tap directly into it as opposed to drawing from an outlet. You may not know from where the outlet obtained its connection or if the connection is contaminated. This can adversely impact you.

What you require in your life is not an outlet; you need to receive from the source itself. The source is Jesus Christ.

God is our source of life. God created this world that we live in. God created everything in the world. Plants, trees, animals, creatures, orbits—every single thing was created by God.

1 Corinthians 6:19

What? Know ye not that your body is the temple of the Holy Ghost which is in you, which ye have of God, and ye are not your own?1 Corinthians 6:19

Watch the question God is asking: "Don't you know that your body is a temple?" Notice the first word: "**What**?"

That first word implies that something happened that shocked and amazed God. Why was He shocked and amazed? Because He expected the Corinthians and today He expects you to know the standard that you, your life, your acts, and your words need to reflect. The moment you fall below that standard, He is amazed, and that's why he exclaims, "What?"

Check the last part of 1 Corinthians 6:19. The Bible says, "You are not your own." If you are not your own, then do all the things that you say you have acquired—certificates, money, houses, businesses, fame, and all other things—belong to you?

If you don't belong to yourself, you are owned by somebody. So how would the things you claim to own be yours? Whoever owns you owns all those things.

Your worship goes beyond the art of just lifting and waving your hands. You should be worshipping God every day throughout your life. This is what you should aspire to do. This is why the Bible says, *In everything give thanks – 1 Thessalonians 5:18.*

However, if you want to offer worship, but deep inside your spirit, you know your mind, heart, and spirit are not there, then don't bother lifting up your hands toward Heaven as a sign of worship. The Bible makes it very clear that making gestures of worship is not worship to Him if your heart, soul, and mind are not in tune with Him. Don't deceive anyone because He sees the heart.

Worship as a result of eye service is worship by men's hands; it's not befitting to God.

God is not begging you to worship Him. God does not need your artificial crying. God does not need your artificial prostrating in church. God does not need your artificial hand clapping. It is not worship to Him. You owe Him worship. It's not His request of you; rather, you owe it to Him. He created you in order that you honor and worship Him. Through your worship, He will bless you and make you great.

He created you for His pleasure. What do you think His pleasure is?

It is not money. It's to worship Him.

He doesn't need your money.

He doesn't need your beauty.

He doesn't need your million-dollar car.

He doesn't need your certificates or position.

All He needs is that you, His temple, come back to Him in worship.

Don't worry too much about your dress when worshipping Him.

Don't worry about your status when worshipping Him.

Your worship is what is required.

Overlooking your mistakes does not exempt you from God's end-time punishment if those mistakes are classified as sin.

Seek the truth and sell it not.

You need to live inside out from now on, if you are not already living that way.

This means if you are worshipping your Maker, your worship needs to be from the inside out.

You start worshipping from within; you start singing songs from inside your spirit before it starts coming out of your mouth to your Maker.

Worship Him inside out, sing inside out, praise Him inside out, and pray from the inside out. In Him, that's inside. Your walking has to be inside out. You live your life inside out.

You need to be able to create from within the job you want, the ideas you want, and the growth you want in your business, career, and home, and then they will come out as a finished product. In Him, we make things happen from the inside.

Most people create things on paper before going to God in prayer. There isn't anything wrong with pre-planning, but I am talking about the principle of Acts 17:28, where you create or request whatever you need from Him. Don't talk about your issue to other people first; talk about it with Him, and you will have your solution.

Give Him your worship today from within you, which is your inside-out worship.

The world often labels people with the wrong identity because of where the person is or what the person may have been doing, saying, wearing, or facing at the time. This has left many people's lives shattered, and we need to be careful that we do not become the cause of someone's destruction, damage, or loss.

You were close to that miracle or job when, all of a sudden, you felt you were a nobody.

You were close to that answer when you overheard someone you trusted say, "It does not work," and you pulled out.

You exchanged contracts, and you suddenly felt very weird and pulled out.

People may not like you for various reasons known only to them.

People may say all sorts of things about you for reasons known only to them.

The devil can throw in wrong motives and reasons why you should not do what you plan to do.

People may react to you the way they do because they see you as a threat.

Don't let anyone or any situation steal your joy, self-confidence, and persistence. You are the most important person to you.

There are so many things that will seek to get your attention, to distract you, to set you back, to challenge you, or to motivate or demotivate you. But you have to know your position and take a stand.

The Bible says "your adversary" the devil. Notice the Bible doesn't say "the adversary," but "your adversary." This tells you that everything wants to fight you, frustrate you, label you, and name you in this life. It is you, not the next person; no wonder the Bible says, *Work out your salvation* – Phillipians 2:12"

Do not panic or be dismayed. No system, force, spirit, or policy can change who God has made and destined you to be.

You are a special person. You were carefully created by God, and your steps are specifically ordered by Him. You are not a cosmic accident. You didn't suddenly just appear on the planet. Even if you don't know your mother or father because she or he left early in your life, it does not matter.

Take these words very seriously: You are not an accident child or individual. You are not a sudden creation. You are not a biological error. Your divine destiny lies in your knowing that God has far better plans for you than your very parents who brought you into this world.

Your awareness of this truth can change your position immediately. Your acceptance of this can take you out of that prison of sickness, that prison of lack, that prison of failure, that prison of inferiority, or that prison of instability.

You are priceless, and God has so much stuff in store for you. As you accept these words, you will see those chains breaking loose from your mind. As you accept these words that are being declared by the Spirit of God, impossibility will become possible, and the change that you have desired for such a long time will come suddenly.

As a woman's water breaks without warning, so also will your miracle happen suddenly—in a flash like thunder. God does not need your permission. All He needs is your rigid faith in Him.

You are special to God, and that is the most important thing in life and in this whole wide world. Don't let anyone tell you otherwise.

You are special to Jehovah. Don't change your confession because God means every word He has spoken concerning you.

God has decorated you, just as a soldier of war is decorated with honour when he has accomplished great and exemplary exploits. God has presented you as a glorious person to the whole world.

CHAPTER SEVEN

THE POWER OF CHOICE

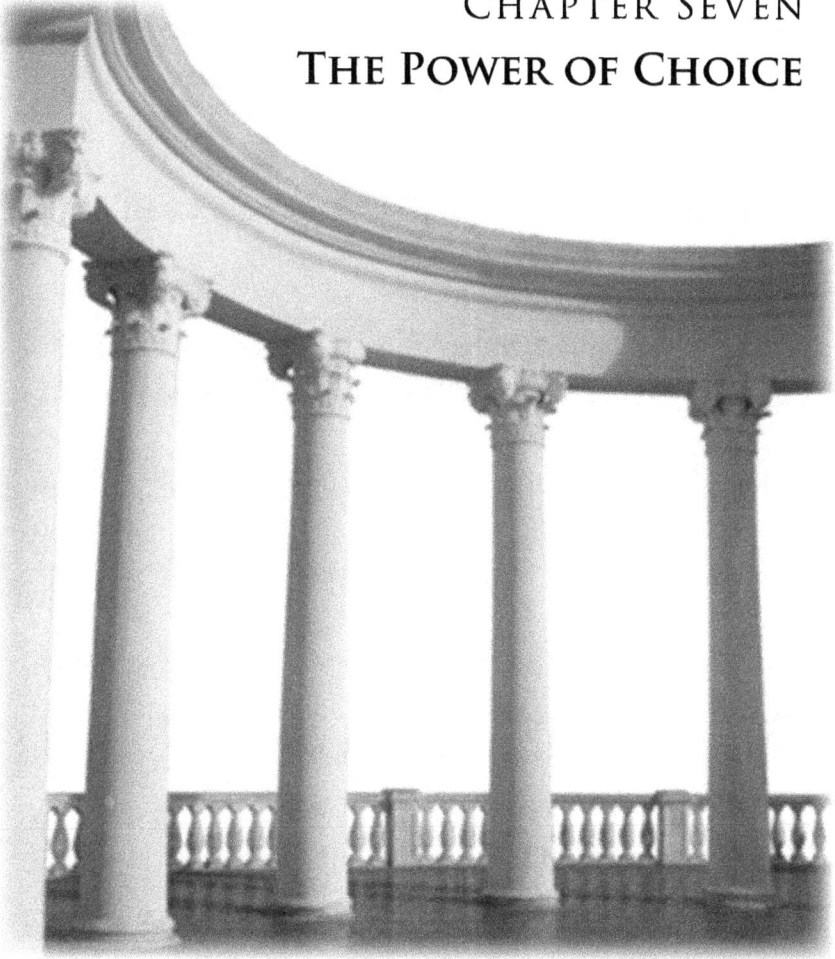

The need to make a choice is crucial. God gave us a will but the use of your will power in determining your choices will make a massive difference.

The foundation of any creation, development, building, business, or empire begins with a conception. This conception is likened to a seed.

From the seed, a child is born. From the seed, a business, idea, dream, or organisation is birthed and nurtured until it becomes a forest.

All seeds, when enhanced, will produce a forest and a harvest.

These seeds have within them all that is needed to reproduce, to expand, to live on, and to be established.

What you do with the seeds in your life, including those seeds in your hands, determines all that happens to you and your posterity in this life and world.

Every person on this planet came into this world with at least one seed, which is the seed of God planted in them. Every individual can have more than one seed that carries all that you need in this world.

Your attention is always required for the sake of your seeds.

Failure to properly nurture the seeds can lead to the infiltration of sinful elements and material, which can impact the growth and life of the seed.

Our duty is to live and work on our seeds until each one of them yields the required results and produces harvest upon harvest.

The moment you lose focus on your seeds, parasites can disturb the growth and life of the seeds.

The problem facing many people today is their inability to identify the weeds in the wheat in their lives.

You have an assignment, and yet you sleep on your duty of assignment. You should not sleep while on duty. The seeds in your hands are connected to your assignment.

Pray that any tares in your life, in your finances, in your marriage, concerning your business, or in your children's life, known and unknown, may be located and duly destroyed. Ask God to send forth His angels to bundle them together and consume them with the fire of the Holy Ghost.

May the seeds in your hands begin to grow and multiply!

My prayer is,

"Let there be roses without thorns,

Life whole without sicknesses and illnesses,

Life without headaches,

Life without lack,

Life without frustrations,

Marriage without divorce and/or separation,

Children without attacks from strange forces,

Hearts without holes,

Lands without ants,

And education, which ensures only success and never any failure."

Whom Do You Listen To?

There are several paths in life, and these paths lead to various destinations. There are various teachers in life, and all of them carry a message, which they deliver to an audience or a group of people.

Many roads can lead you where you want to go in life, and knowing the right one to follow is important in achieving your desired result. If you follow the wrong road or go the wrong direction, you can wind up in a great catastrophe.

In life there are people who speak to us on a daily basis. But how do you identify whom to listen to and whose advice to take? How can you discern who genuinely has your interests at heart when he or she is speaking to you, giving you a piece of advice, or giving you some direction?

This opens you to danger and vulnerability. The voice you listen to can either make you or mar you. The voice you listen to can mean the difference between success and failure. The voice you listen to can make the difference between starting well and not starting at all.

In order for you to be assured that every step you take is correct, and every decision you make is accurate, and every activity you engage in is accomplished perfectly, you need something or someone who knows everything in this world.

You need an insider, someone who knows all about today, the events of tomorrow, and the outcome of any events to come, and knows *you* very well. How many people can you find on this earth who fit this description?

I have searched the world, reviewed all manner of history books, and surfed the World Wide Web, and no other person was named except the one who is the third person of the trinity: the Holy Spirit.

The fundamental difference between having any spirit and having the Holy Spirit is that the Holy Spirit is not only a spirit, which is invisible, but He has a personality, which makes Him powerful beyond all other spirits.

For you to have the life that you have always desired, you will need the Holy Spirit with you throughout the whole of life's journey.

The number-one thing for you to do to see transformation in your life is to believe and acknowledge that the Holy Spirit exists.

Count yourself worthy of having the opportunity to communicate with such a divine personality.

The Holy Spirit translates God's messages concerning you in a manner that you can understand and relate to.

The Holy Spirit is a communicator.

The Holy Spirit is the medium of communication between us and God and between you and the trinity.

The Holy Spirit is your representative in Heaven's counsel.

The Holy Spirit is the independent counsellor who is allowed to represent you and talk on your behalf in Heaven, but at the same time, He is equally allowed to talk on your behalf here on earth.

What you need daily is a word from the Holy Spirit.

You can only know His voice, His personality, and His ways if you have fellowship with Him. Entering fellowship with Him allows you to know His voice and ways. This means your living with him continuously and becoming acquainted with Him, His voice, and His movements.

A sweet aroma is associated with Him. Just as every individual has a fragrance associated with him or her, the Holy Spirit as a person has one. With the Holy Spirit

Your presence is that element that is classified as your identity and authenticity. You cannot be separate from your presence and person.

Don't panic about Satan and his activity, but rather rejoice in the authority of your Father, who is omnipotent (all power and authority), omnipresent, and omniscient. Seek that presence because it can be with you everywhere.

You must know when the presence of God is available and know how to react to the presence of God.

Not knowing His presence will mean the difference between missing your miracle and getting it.

The presence of God should attract you more than anything else. Reduce visits to your friends and colleagues, and make new appointments with and visits to the presence of God.

His presence brings you answers. There is wholeness in His presence. There is a grace in His presence that makes up for any shortfall.

Anytime you try to avoid God's presence, you will face unnecessary problems and become a burden on people.

Avoiding God's presence is denying yourself great blessings.

dwelling in you and working with you in everything, you can never be disadvantaged in this world.

His presence and companionship are the greatest armor you can have in life. His indwelling is the greatest gift any person can receive.

The antidote to life's worries, issues, concerns, or challenges is the Holy Spirit. When you have Him, you have an immediate power to counteract the problem.

Sickness, disease, challenges, problems, anxiety, and worries cannot dwell in the same place with the Holy Spirit.

He will tell you everything you need to know about life and the future. He is more than a resource point; He is the answer to all of your life's questions here on earth.

Every word spoken by the Holy Spirit is an instruction from God the Father.

In Whose Presence Are You?

Every human being carries a presence with him or her. You have your own presence as a person.

Your presence symbolises some essential traits of your personality. The sum total of your personality, when displayed, personifies your presence.

His presence is all you need to keep your marriage from falling apart. His presence is all you need to give your business some great returns on your investments. His presence is all you need to bring the needed peace to your home.

Create an atmosphere that welcomes His presence and see how things begin to change for you.

CHAPTER EIGHT
THE POWER OF NAMES

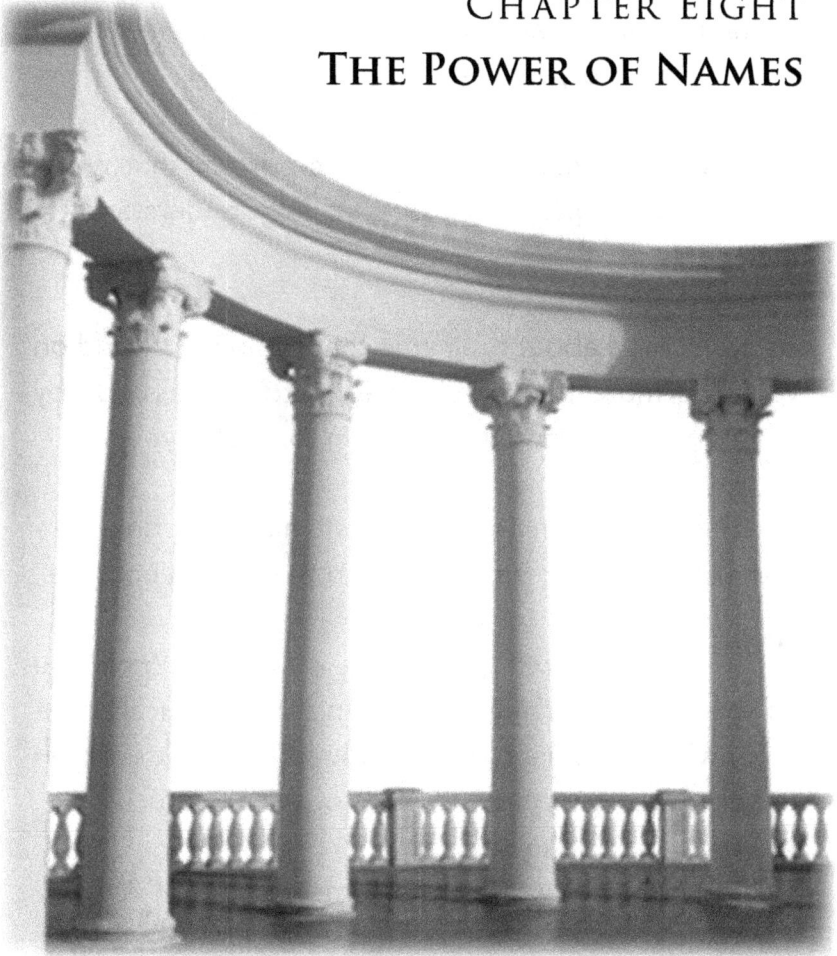

Names are vital in everyday life. Knowing a name helps you to locate the person or place you are looking for. Names therefore carry with them identity.

Your name identifies you. Names represent life. Names represent success or failure. Names represent death or life. A name that you take upon yourself or that someone has given you affects you and everything that pertains to your life.

Names have meanings, and it's important that whatever name is given to you, you fully understand its meaning.

Be concerned about the name that has been placed on you. The more that person begins to address you by that name, very soon it may begin to impact you.

The name of a person or place will have a lasting, permanent impression and impact on the person or place.

You will always be remembered by your name. When you go to a museum, a memorial, or an archaeological site, it is not what the person did that you will see written upon the plaques, but rather the name of the person.

Everything in this world has a name associated with it.

When challenges come and the economies of the world struggle, the economist and governments label it "an economic crisis," "financial meltdown," "credit crunch," or "recession." The more they refer to these names, the more the action occurs. So when the economy needs to grow, the growth stagnates because people are still saying financial dip.

When a swelling comes upon a person's body, doctors call it "a growth," "an abscess," or "an inflammation;"

these then manifest themselves with their peculiar features.

When your body begins to feel uncomfortable with a burning sensation to your head and body, they call it "a headache," "the flu," etc. All these are names, and they all impact people's lives.

Doctors then introduce you to the name "Neurofen" or "Paracetamol," which will take away the thing called headache.

Despite whatever state you may be in now—be it stress, unemployment, hardship, lack, failure, setback, worries, sickness—whatever the name, I introduce to you the name Jesus Christ.

I introduce to you the name of Jesus. The Bible says at the mention of that name, whatever your situation, whatever the problem, whatever the question, whatever the challenge, His name will bring you an answer; His name will bring you a cure; His name will bring you a resolution and a release, healing and breakthrough. Simply, it is "In the name of Jesus."

He is the Son of God, and He is the ancient of days. Before eternity existed, he existed.

Before anything could be called something, He existed, hence the Bible says, "*at the mention of his name Jesus, Phillipians 2:10*" all things come under subjection.

You need the name of Jesus to save that marriage.

You need the name of Jesus to save you from that sickness.

You need the name of Jesus to bring you peace in that home.

This is the only name that shall not be destroyed.

All other names shall pass away and fade.

The Name of Jesus

Many people have come and gone. Many names have made national and international headlines, but they are no more.

Many people have won the hearts of men and women, boys and girls around the world with their names, but today they are no more. The only name that has maintained its efficacy and strength and continues forever is the name of Jesus.

The starting point of your life and the ability to live it to the fullest is your faith in the name of Jesus.

If you believe in the name of Jesus, no matter the decomposed nature of your situation or circumstance, and no matter the magnitude of what you need, you can have it. It begins by believing in the name of Jesus. You will have true life.

If you call on Jesus today, wherever you are reading this, no matter what the sin is, even if you have done some abominable things, have acted in some unspeakable ways, and been in the company of the most undeserved, it does not make a difference to God. His arms are always open wide, and He is ready to receive you.

The Holy Spirit, when received within, will guide you into all truth. With the Holy Spirit directing the affairs of your life, you will never make a mistake or miss out on anything. He is the master strategist.

That power in the name of Jesus is greater than the biggest reservoir of electricity in the world. The electrical current within the name of Jesus is greater than any current or innovation that will ever be created.

His name is His surety. When you mention the name of Jesus, you do not need any other surety. His name is also your surety for your future, which is eternal life.

The name Jesus equals "answer." Jesus is the answer to all of life's questions.

Stop calling on the medicine. Stop calling on the prescription. Stop calling on the lawyers. Stop calling on the bank manager. Change the situation today. Start calling on the name of Jesus, and you will receive the healing and answers you need.

Anything and everything you require is wrapped up in the Word of God in the name of Jesus.

You can have it if you can believe and call on that name, Jesus.

At the mention of the name of Jesus, your current situation and status can change.

At the mention of that name, life can turn around for you in the blink of an eye.

Your obedience in accepting this truth and participating in the call of worship will bring the answers and solutions you have wanted.

At the mention of His name, lives are transformed.

At the mention of His name, any dead situation in your life will resurrect again.

At the mention of His name, barriers are broken down.

At the mention of His name, cancer disappears.

At the mention of His name, debts are canceled and financial giants are raised.

At the mention of His name, miracles take place.

At the mention of His name, the earth and the whole world shake.

At the mention of His name, everything created in this world responds.

At the mention of His name, you will be free from bondage.

At the mention of His name, any form of sickness or disease disappears.

His name is all that you need.

In the mighty name of Jesus Christ.

CHAPTER NINE

SIGNS AND ABUNDANCE

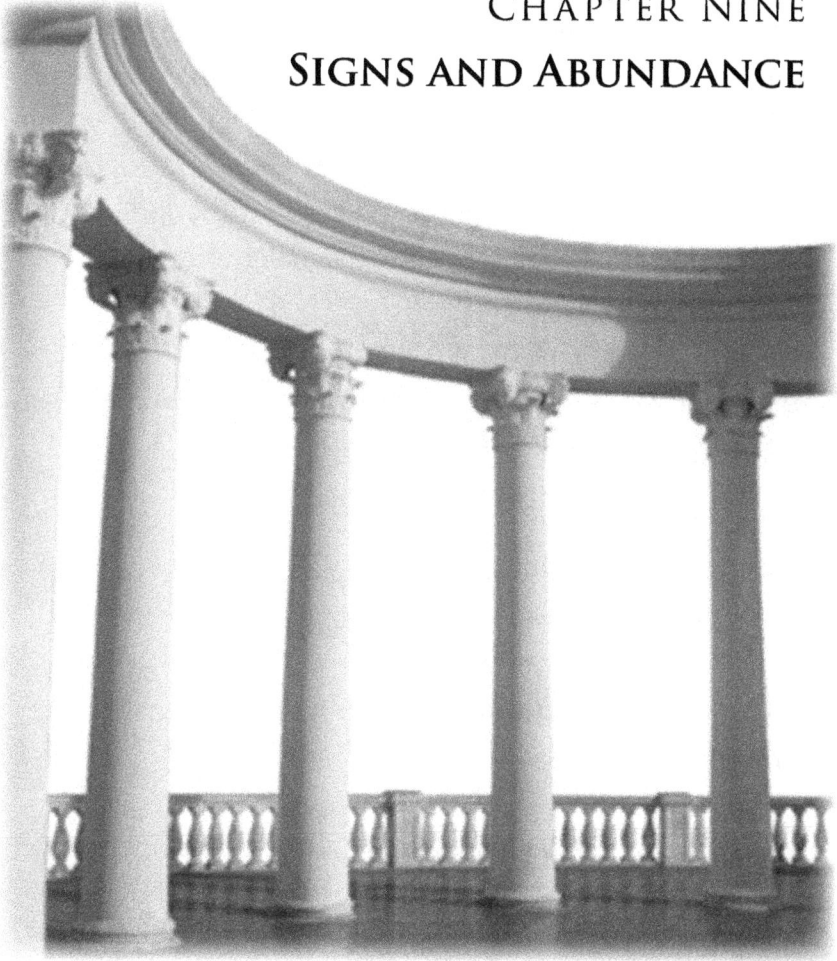

I t is not good to just make do with your existing state of affairs.

Your situation and current state of affairs can be changed, amplified, and multiplied for the better for your life and generations to come.

When God amplifies your being and existence, your enemies run away before you arrive in person because your spirit and ability go way ahead of you.

Addition is an activity triggered by you, the individual. Addition is triggered by your personal efforts.

Multiplication is increase. Increase is an activity triggered by a supernatural authority without your involvement. Increase refers to unaided growth.

Adding is natural.

Multiplying them is supernatural.

Multiplying, therefore, requires ability and capability greater than you.

Your prayer needs to change from "God, please add to the wealth in my hand" to "God, please multiply the wealth in my hand."

Multiplication is continuous, unending.

Don't focus only on your skills. Don't focus only on your network of friends. Don't keep dreaming of how different you could have made what you do. Be focussed, don't try strategising with a million routes.

The center of attraction for you to get to the next stage, or for your plans to get to the next level, will not be you or your plans. The center of focus has to be God.

Realign your strategy, go back to God, and ask for the blessing of amplification and multiplication.

God's ability is faster than any organic system. He is quicker than a microwave or the speed of light.

Just having people support your idea does not mean your model is correct.

I am waiting to know, making do with what I have until I get the new one; but the problem is I am not sure of what will happen next from this position.

Many people have lived their lives around this human baseline.

The problem today is that, even some Christians cannot be excused from the status quo.

When God shows a sign of what is about to come to you, it gives you a sense of direction. It supports your plans and strategies concerning what you are doing and how you will continue to do it.

Your prayer today is, "Dear Lord, show me the sign that I am looking for. As the thunder signifies the coming of a storm, may You, O God, give me a sign for the prayer request and for the miracle I am expecting."

If you are tired of your present status, ask God to grant you fresh position and, according to His Word, the **sign of increase**.

Sometimes the sign God gives you will be from within the circumstance you are in. Don't necessarily run away from the storm with your eyes closed. When that challenge comes to you, pray and watch carefully because in the face of that challenge lies the sign.

The answer in most cases gravitates around the problem.

If you are asking for a sign because you doubt God, be very careful, because God is not answerable to you. You must go to Him knowing that He is who He is.

Whenever the sign comes, it helps you avoid unnecessary choices and deviations.

The sign from God will take you to the next higher place where your miracle is awaiting you.

Your location is very crucial in the search for where you are going or for what you are doing.

Without a spiritual compass and divine coordinates being plotted for you from Heaven, you can keep going around and around and around, and you may not locate the exact thing you are asking for.

A sign from God is all that you need. God is still in the business of giving signs.

It's your turn today. You will receive a sign from God.

You must pray to God to gain spiritual understanding in order to be able to locate the spiritual sign always given by God before it metamorphoses into the physical.

Whenever God gives a sign, the indication of which concerns your particular situation, the sign, which is first released in Spirit, is now identified in the physical. So instead of mistakenly preempting the evidence of what we are expecting, let's seek to grow more in Him so we can pick up the sign from the Spirit and act on the sign for our final result.

Seeing early enough the sign in the realm of the Spirit would also take you faster to your desired results and expectations. It is faster than the physical sign.

By reaching for your sign in the Spirit world on your knees in prayer before it comes out in the open, you save time.

Don't wait for the physical sign of God before you act. The moment you take the matter to God, God releases it in the realm of the Spirit to you.

Believe it, receive it, and it's yours.

Your status will change with the sign of God.

Don't relax in your old status; don't stay in the position that you were in before the sign of God came. Don't stay in the mind-set of that position any more.

The moment you see the sign of God, don't live the past life. Be mindful of your new status and walk in the revelation of it.

Be thankful to God for the sign. The moment you receive it, start running with the benefits that accompany the sign and claim and walk in them. They are your Heaven-approved promises by God Himself.

Your answers have been given already; accept and believe this fact; they are yours and walk in them. Amen.

Words of Power (Powerful Confessions)

I am a winner.

I am prosperous.

I am the best among my peers.

I am blessed.

I live in abundance.

I have all things.

I am the healed of the Lord.

I succeed in all that I do.

This is my set time.

I will not fail.

I will not be defeated.

I operate with a different set of rules.

My mind-set is the mind-set of God.

My mind-set is the mind-set of the righteous.

My mind-set is that of a perpetual winner.

I have sufficient ability because I tap directly from the source.

This is my blessing.

I do not struggle in life.

Nothing is difficult for me because of Jesus in me.

I am strong; I have peace.

I am born of God. I am encouraged; I am strengthened.

My life is not a gamble; I am living the good life, pre-planned for me by God.

I am the righteousness of God in Christ Jesus.

I am the best in everything I do. I am a victor.

I am winning all the way.

Nothing can change my course.

I am on the path of greatness, success, and liberty.

I enjoy God's peace and blessings.

I am blessed because I cannot be disadvantaged.

My mind is made up.

I am an offspring of divinity. My citizenship is in Heaven.

I am faithful to my Maker.

I am a wise person because I am winning souls for Christ.

I cannot be stopped by any infirmity or sickness.

I have the very life of God inside me.

Today is my time, moment, and season of blessings.

I will not be a reproach.

I am a blessing wherever I go. I am blessed and very highly favored.

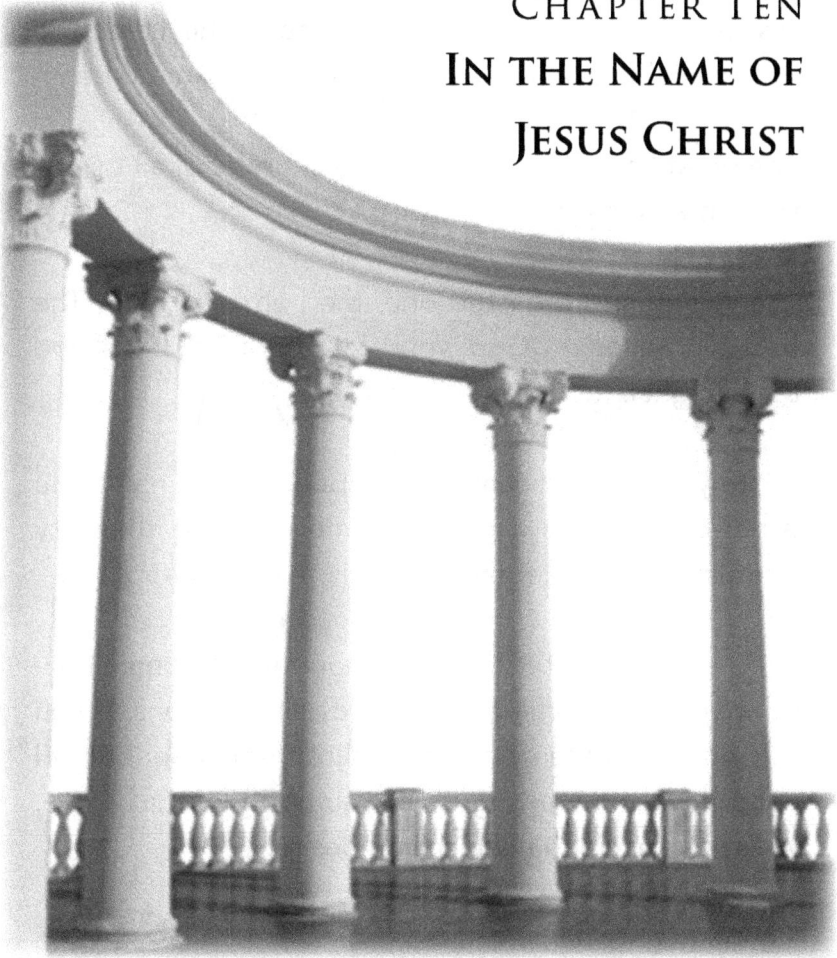

The name "Jesus" equals "answer." Jesus is answer.

At the mention of His name, everything created in this world responds to his name.

His name is ominpotent, ever present, the Lord who knows all things and is everywhere at the same time.

The great I am, the majestic king, the ruler of all things, His name is Jesus.

The strong and breasted one, the I am that I am. The true counsellor, my God, your God, our God. He is God the almighty.

When you call that name, He responds to his name. He is not dead, He is alive, the name is bigger than any trouble you can ever face.

The name is greater than any mountain that may confront you. The name that changes all situations. If you can remember the name and not just remember but call upon that name relying on the authority of that name, you can achieve that which you desire.

"In the mighty name of Jesus Christ."

CONCLUSION

I trust that God has blessed you and imparted to you some great knowledge, revelations, directions, and blessings.

I trust that this first volume of *Words of Wisdom* has given you some support and benefit.

My prayer for you is that in your quest in life, you will continue to seek the truth and build up more and more in all that you know.

In conclusion, the Bible states, *Wisdom is a shelter as money is a shelter, but the advantage of knowledge is this: Wisdom preserves those who have it.* Ecclesiastes 7:12 (NIV)

God bless you.

For ministering appointments, lectures, conference talks, concerts, and any other requests, contact the following:

Rev. Addo Anyani-Boadum
Jesus Generation Ministries UK
Centre of Excellence
443 Streatham High Road
London
SW16 3PH.
Tel: +44(0)203 632 8986
E-mail: pastor@jesusgeneration.co.uk
info@changinglivesproject.com
Website: addoanyaniboadum.org

www.ingramcontent.com/pod-product-compliance
Lightning Source LLC
Chambersburg PA
CBHW072009060426
42446CB00042B/2255